Bodies from the Ice

Melting Glaciers and the Recovery of the Past

www.houghtonmifflinbooks.com

The book design is by YAY! Design.
The text of this book is set in Meridien.
Maps by Jerry Malone

Library of Congress Cataloging-in-Publication Data
Deem, James M.
Bodies from the ice: melting glaciers and the
recovery of the past / by James M. Deem.
     p.cm.
ISBN 978-0-618-80045-2
     1. Ice mummies—Juvenile literature.
     2. Otzi (Ice mummy)—Juvenile literature.
     I. Title.

GN293.D43 2008
599.9—dc22

2008001868

Printed in China
WKT 10 9 8 7 6 5 4 3 2 1

Illustration credits appear on page 57.

Bodies from the Ice

Melting Glaciers and the Recovery of the Past

by James M. Deem

HOUGHTON MIFFLIN COMPANY
Boston 2008

Contents

1. Iceman of the Alps 1

2. Grinding, Gliding Glaciers 9

3. Dragons in the Ice 17

4. Frozen Children of the Andes 27

5. The Mystery of Mallory 35

6. Another Man from a Glacier 43

7. Saving the Past 49

54 Glaciers to Visit and Suggested Websites

55 Acknowledgments and Bibliography

57 Illustration Credits

58 Index

This 1826 aquatint by the Swiss artist Samuel Birmann shows the power of the De Bois Glacier near Chamonix, France. As ice melted in higher areas of the glacier, it drained and formed a large channel of water at its base, creating an icy cavern some 150 feet in height. This is the source of France's Arveyron River.

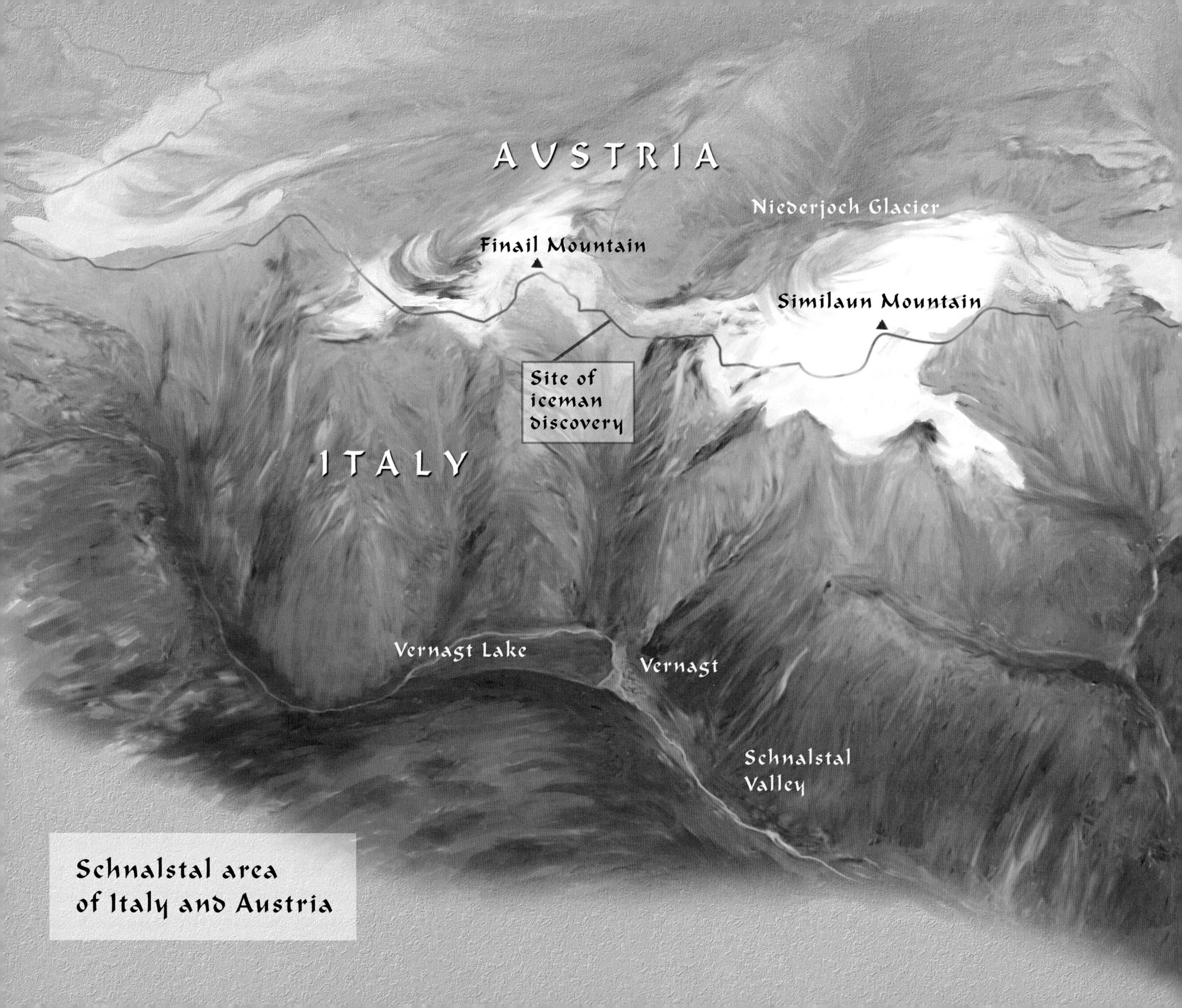

AUSTRIA

Niederjoch Glacier

Finail Mountain ▲

Similaun Mountain ▲

Site of
iceman
discovery

ITALY

Vernagt Lake

Vernagt

Schnalstal
Valley

Schnalstal area
of Italy and Austria

CHAPTER 1

Iceman of the Alps

O n the morning of September 18, 1991, while on vacation in northern Italy, Erika and Helmut Simon decided to climb the Similaun, a twelve-thousand-foot-high mountain near the Austrian border. They had scaled the peak once before, in 1981, but this time the journey would be much more challenging.

To reach the summit, the couple had to cross part of the Niederjoch Glacier, which had once deeply covered much of the nearby mountains. Although the Niederjoch had been gradually retreating, or thawing, since 1850, its melting, like that of many other glaciers around the world, had greatly accelerated since 1981. Snowfall had been lighter, and summer temperatures had been higher. Not only did the new snow melt each summer, but the once-permanent glacier ice thawed as well.

By 1991, after an especially warm summer, the glacier that remained, which may have been more than sixty feet deep in

A man's well-preserved body was discovered in the melting remains of the Niederjoch Glacier in the Ötztal Alps. The red circle identifies the spot.

the 1920s, was only three feet deep in some places and quite slushy in the heat. Still, wide gaps or fissures in the ice, called *crevasses*, sliced deeply through other areas. One misstep and the Simons could easily fall into a crevasse and be gravely, even fatally, injured. As a result, they climbed cautiously, taking much longer to reach the summit than they expected.

When they were ready to return to their hotel in the valley below, it was almost dark and too dangerous to continue their descent. Forced to spend the night in a mountain lodge, they were not happy about their rustic accommodations; they had no running water or indoor toilet. The next day, though, they would learn how truly lucky they were: the melting of the Niederjoch Glacier allowed them to make one of the most important archaeological discoveries of all time.

The next morning, they climbed another nearby mountain, the Finail, where a hiker could stand with one foot in Austria and the other in Italy. After reaching the summit, the Simons were eager to return to their comfortable hotel. On their way down, they crossed a portion of the Niederjoch Glacier that had melted away dramatically, exposing a rocky terrain.

There they noticed something unexpected in the slushy ice of a rocky gully. At first, Helmut thought it was trash left behind by a careless hiker. But as they approached, his wife realized what they had stumbled upon.

"It's a person," she said.

They stopped a few feet away.

In front of them a body lay face-down in a patch of melting ice.

Without a word, they both quickly stepped onto a ledge above the gully where they could get a better, safer view of the body, its shoulders and upper back bare. The rest of the corpse was encased in what was left of the glacial ice.

Despite his wife's protests, Helmut took a photograph of the body. He figured that the person must have died in a mountain accident and that relatives might want to see a photo of where the body was found. Then the

ABOVE LEFT:
When excavators finally reached the glacier corpse, snow again covered the body.

ABOVE RIGHT:
The body was removed from the gully by a police officer and a professor of forensic medicine.

Perhaps the most important item that the Iceman carried was his ax. Some two feet long, it was made from a piece of yew tree, using a sturdy branch that grew out of the trunk. The handle was fashioned from the trunk, while the shaft (the part onto which the copper blade was fitted) was shaped from the branch. Such a natural joint allowed the ax to be both strong and durable.

The copper blade was fitted into the shaft and wrapped with a leather binding; the binding was coated with birch tar. The three-inch shaft was forked at the end, and the blade extended out of the leather binding about one inch.

Scientists reconstructed his ax to see how it compared to a modern one. They discovered that the ax would have required more effort to use: three swings of the Iceman's ax equaled one swing from a modern version. Still, a woodcutter was able to chop down a yew tree using the ax in forty-five minutes.

The ax is the only complete one from the Copper Age ever discovered.

couple headed off to report their discovery.

At first, authorities thought that the corpse had been discovered on the Austrian side, and Austrian police were not surprised that a body had turned up in the glacier. Five corpses had already been recovered that year in their country's glaciers, including the bodies of a couple missing since 1934. Now that the glaciers were melting, the bodies of long-missing hikers and mountaineers were turning up with regularity. In fact, Austrian authorities initially suspected that the body might be that of a music professor who had disappeared on a hike in 1938.

When the police inspector saw the body two days later, however, he realized that this corpse might be a bit different. First, some scraps of fur, string, and wood were found on the ledge near the body along with an unusual ax, all of which suggested to the inspector that the body might have come from the 1800s. Second, the inspector was surprised to see an almost complete, mummified body. When hikers or climbers died in glacier accidents, often by falling into crevasses, their bodies were frequently battered and sometimes pulverized by the moving glacier ice; many such bodies ended

Ötzi was displayed to reporters shortly after his discovery. Scientists were fascinated by his very advanced two-part shoes, the oldest ones ever found (he wears a shoe on his right foot). The upper part was made from a netting of the dried inner bark of a lime tree, covered in deerskin, stuffed with hay, and laced up to keep the moisture out. It was stitched with a leather strap to the oval bearskin sole.

up decomposed and reduced to bits of bone.

Although the inspector wondered if the person had been murdered, he decided not to treat the recovery of the body as a crime scene. The belongings indicated that if it were a crime, it had been committed more than a hundred years earlier, far too long ago to solve. For this reason, few photographs were taken, and objects near the body were removed without recording their original location. The first excavators even used a mini-jackhammer to help free the body; the drill dug into the frozen flesh on the corpse's hip, badly damaging it. What's more, when the ax was taken to the local police station, the commanding officer scratched the blade with his car keys to determine what metal had been used. A few days later, after archaeologists were finally called to the site, a long stick found in the ice near the body was pried out carelessly and it snapped in two.

By the time the body was transported to the medical examiner for an autopsy, reporters from local newspapers and television stations had begun to ask questions. They speculated excitedly that the person might have died as many as five hundred years earlier. One thing became quite clear: when Italian officials surveyed the discovery area, they realized that the corpse had been found just inside the Italian border, and they wanted the body back. But the results of radiocarbon testing a few weeks later revealed a much greater surprise: the corpse from the melting ice

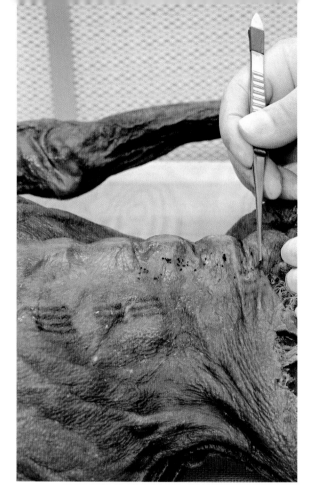

Ötzi's body was covered with some fifty-nine bluish black tattoos made with powdered charcoal. Shaped like lines and crosses, they are perhaps the first evidence of acupuncture, used to relieve pain in highly stressed parts of his body (his lower back, his right knee, his left calf, and his ankle joints).

Almost a year after the discovery, archaeologists conducted a thorough excavation of Ötzi's discovery site. They retrieved his bearskin cap, a fingernail, and some strands of hair.

was a man who had lived 5,300 years earlier, during the Copper Age. He was the oldest human mummy ever found preserved by freezing.

His recovery from the ice, however, had damaged not only his body but some of his possessions. For example, the long stick that was snapped in half was an ancient longbow, and somehow the wooden frame of his backpack was broken into pieces. Reportedly, people who had passed by the discovery site before the body was excavated had even helped themselves to a few souvenirs. And it wasn't until almost a year later that a thorough excavation of the discovery site was completed.

As Italy pressed for the return of the body, the ancient man needed an official name for legal documents. An Austrian scientist proposed Hauslabjoch Man, for the closest geographic place name (a mountain pass) to the location of the corpse. Many other names were suggested as well, including the Iceman. But another name, given by an Austrian newspaper, stuck: Ötzi (rhymes with *tootsie*), for the Ötztal Alps where he had been found. Eventually he was returned to Italy. There, scientists and researchers from around the world studied Ötzi and his possessions, which provided an extraordinary window into the distant past of the Copper Age.

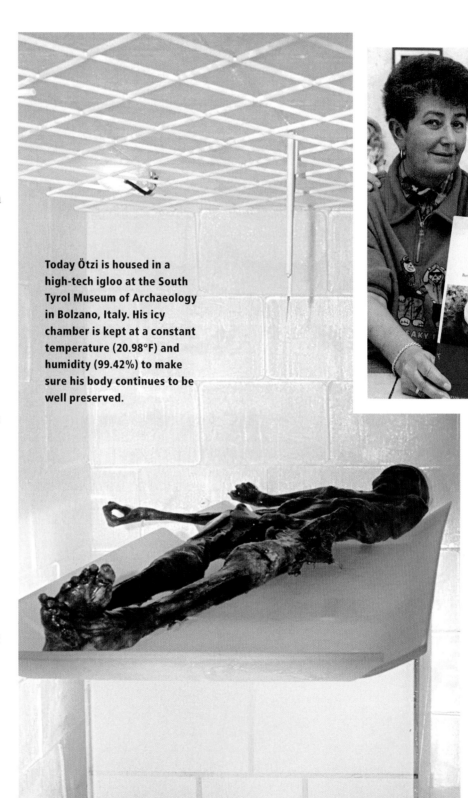

Today Ötzi is housed in a high-tech igloo at the South Tyrol Museum of Archaeology in Bolzano, Italy. His icy chamber is kept at a constant temperature (20.98°F) and humidity (99.42%) to make sure his body continues to be well preserved.

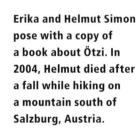

Erika and Helmut Simon pose with a copy of a book about Ötzi. In 2004, Helmut died after a fall while hiking on a mountain south of Salzburg, Austria.

The Iceman's Death

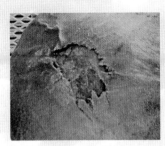

Ötzi's back reveals two injuries: one to his head (close-up above), caused by a blow, and another to his hip (below), caused by careless excavators.

Early researchers theorized that, caught in a sudden snowstorm, Ötzi fell asleep and froze to death. Others thought that he might have been injured in a fight or a fall before he froze. While some x-rays suggested that he had broken ribs, others did not reveal any broken bones in his abdomen.

In June 2001, almost ten years after Ötzi's discovery, a team of scientists discovered an arrowhead embedded in his left shoulder. A year later, wounds were found on his right hand and wrist. In 2003, another researcher analyzed some of Ötzi's clothing and weapons for signs of blood and found the DNA of four other people. These revelations led to another conclusion: Ötzi had died from an arrow wound after fighting for his life.

In 2007, another team of scientists added one more piece of information after they examined an injury on the back of Ötzi's head, long supposed to have been caused by exposure to the sun when the body emerged from the ice. Their analysis revealed that although the arrow did cause severe damage, he was actually killed when someone struck him on the head shortly after the arrow had pierced his shoulder.

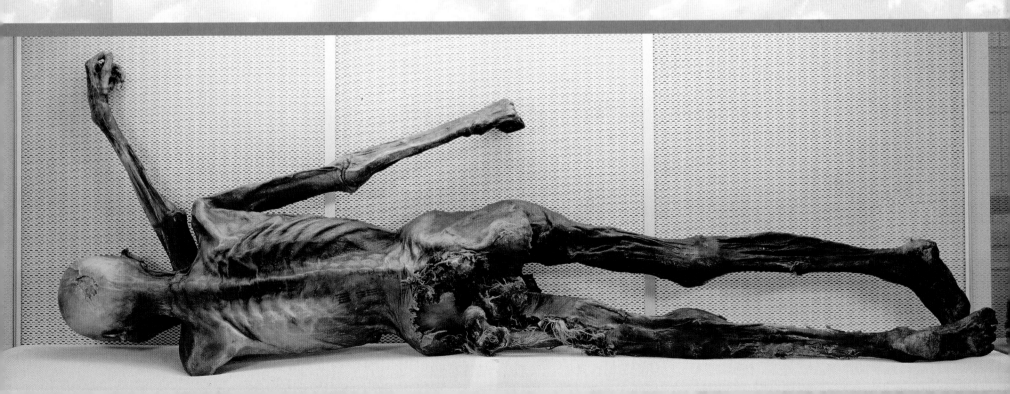

CHAPTER 2

Grinding, Gliding Glaciers

The Theodul Glacier is located in Italy south of Switzerland's famed Matterhorn, seen in the distance on the right. The remains of a soldier were found on the melting edge of the glacier over a period of four years.

Although he is the oldest human found in the remains of an alpine glacier, Ötzi is not the only preserved person discovered under such conditions. Many other bodies—those of hunters, soldiers, shepherds, mountain climbers, and unfortunate travelers—have been recovered both before and after the Simons' finding in 1991. And since glacier ice can preserve objects made from wood, metal, and animal horn, as well as most types of clothing, many historical artifacts have also turned up.

But researchers wanted to know how Ötzi had become so well preserved, even down to his eyeballs. Other frozen corpses found in glaciers were usually from no more than a few hundred years ago.

Types of Glaciers

Ice Sheets and Ice Caps

The largest glacier areas, primarily in Greenland and Antarctica, account for about 95 percent of the glacial ice found on Earth.

Ice Shelves

These floating areas of glacier ice, mostly found in Antarctica, create icebergs.

Alpine Glaciers

These glaciers, found at high elevations, can cover a mountain, an entire mountain range, or even a volcano. If they are contained within a hollow area on a mountainside, they are called *cirque glaciers*. If they spill downhill into valleys, they are named *valley glaciers*. Almost all archaeological finds are made in alpine glaciers.

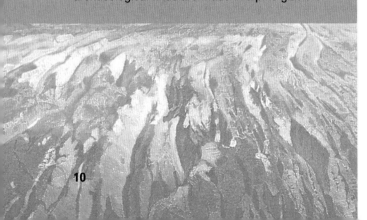

This rocky depression below the moving ice helped preserve Ötzi for 5,300 years. The red dot indicates the location of the body.

After examining the body, scientists concluded that Ötzi had been naturally mummified within a few months of his death. Pollen from the blossoms of the hophornbeam tree found in his intestine revealed that he probably died in the spring, when the still-cold temperatures on the mountain could temporarily preserve his body. The summer after his death, the gully in which the body lay filled with cold water as the snow melted. This caused the outer layer of his skin to peel off and his body to float perhaps a few yards away from its original position. By the end of the summer, when the water had drained, the fluids inside Ötzi's body evaporated in the sun, which further safeguarded him from decomposing. That fall and winter, his body was buried under snowfall that eventually turned into a glacier, sealing him under the ice and preserving him for 5,300 years.

But that still didn't explain why Ötzi had remained almost completely intact for

so long; other glacier corpses are almost always found in pieces. Scientists know that an alpine glacier is formed when more snow accumulates on a mountain than can melt during the summer. Usually after one year, the unmelted snow becomes a dense, hard ice called *firn*. If this process continues for a few years, firn turns into a mass of larger ice crystals, and a glacier is created.

Once formed, the glacier becomes a giant conveyor belt—essentially a moving river of ice—with two main parts: a higher *accumulation* area and a lower *ablation* (or melting) area. Although snow accumulates and melts in both parts, the accumulation area (where more snow falls than melts) pressures the glacier ice to advance to the ablation area (where more snow melts). The glacier not only moves downhill, but it also carries rocks and other debris, both on and below the surface.

Scientists didn't understand why Ötzi's buried body didn't move with the glacier. They knew that when a climber dies by falling into a crevasse, the ice gradually transports the body to the glacier's *snout,* or the lowest point of the ablation zone. As the body moves,

The white snow of Switzerland's Glärnisch Glacier is the accumulation zone, while the darker, gray area is where ablation, or melting, takes place. The snout is the lowest point of the ablation zone. The photo of this cirque glacier was taken in 1982; a photo taken today would reveal a very different glacier, one with little or no accumulation zone and a very large ablation area.

The snout of the advancing Crusoe Glacier on Canada's Axel Heilberg Island (near Greenland) is quite steep. Because of its small size, it is continuing to advance, unaffected for now by changes in the earth's climate.

the weight and the pressure of the ice usually crush it to bits.

When scientists examined the gully where Ötzi was found, they observed that the rocky depression had protected his body from the gliding ice. Had he died outside the trench, his body would have moved with the glacier and been pulverized on its way to the snout.

What's more, his trip would have taken far less than 5,300 years.

How much less time? some researchers wondered.

Although every glacier advances at its own speed, its velocity depends on how much ice is melting, how steep the mountain is, how thick the glacier is, and what type of terrain lies beneath the glacier. Researchers can determine glacier speeds scientifically, but one informal and quite gruesome measure of how fast a glacier travels is the time it takes the body of a person who falls into a glacier to arrive at its snout.

The archaeologist Konrad Spindler tells the story of three people—two men and a

woman—crossing the Madatsch Glacier in the Tyrolean Alps in August 1923. The woman died when she fell into a crevasse so deep that her body could not be retrieved. Then the woman's body traveled with the glacier and resurfaced in a *moraine,* or debris field, at the snout. In all, her body had moved only one thousand feet from the site of her death, but it took twenty-nine years to do so.

That may have been a relatively speedy trip, however, since the archaeologist Harald Stadler reports that glacier corpses in the

Alps can resurface much more slowly, often between one hundred and two hundred years later, because of the soil conditions beneath the glacier.

One body that took almost four hundred years to resurface was found in 1985 in the melting Theodul Glacier along the Swiss-Italian border. That summer, a skier had noticed a few old coins and a small knife on the snout of the glacier. Later that fall, a thorough search uncovered thirty-five coins, some cloth, leather pieces from some boots—and a human thighbone. Excavators also found bones and teeth from two mules or horses.

Snowfall ended the excavation; when it continued in September 1986, searchers were surprised by the dramatic change in the glacier. So much had disappeared that many objects were now lying on the surface of the shallow ice: ninety additional coins, including two that clearly dated from the reign of King Phillip II of Spain (1556–1598), and an astonishing sword with a broken blade. The next year, a pistol and a dagger were retrieved along with the top part of a human skull. The next two years revealed only some scattered coins or small scraps of cloth or metal. By 1990 the glacier had completely retreated from the area,

The unusual sword, more than four feet long, may have been made by a German blacksmith and would have been used by a mounted military officer.

The soles of the soldier's boots, made from a number of thin layers of leather, were recovered from the ice early in the excavations.

Some two hundred copper coins were gathered, including nine large silver ones.

When it was discovered, the soldier's wet skull, its calcium leached by the glacier ice, was soft and spongy. It hardened after it dried.

and no other discoveries were made.

As scientists studied the artifacts, they began to fill in the details of the life and death of the man from the Theodul Glacier. The preserved scalp on his skull told them that he had brown hair. His bones and teeth revealed that he was between thirty-five and forty-five years old when he died. The length of his thighbone indicated that he had stood about five and a half feet tall. The dates on thirteen coins found near the body suggested that he died around 1595. And his fancy new boots and finely made clothing implied that he was a soldier or military officer, most likely on his way to fight for the king of Spain as a paid mercenary.

As for his cause of death, scientists suspected that he might have crossed a snow bridge that collapsed under the weight of the man and his pack animals. They concluded that he became a skeleton because he died in the summer when temperatures were too warm to preserve him. During the next four centuries, the glacier's ice pressed against his skeleton, breaking it into parts as it was carried toward the snout.

In the end, scientists realized that Ötzi's preservation was caused by a special set of circumstances, making the discovery of another ancient glacier corpse quite unlikely. If he had not been sheltered, his body parts would have resurfaced in no more than a few hundred years. Then, lying at the edge of the ice, Ötzi's remains would have quickly decomposed and disappeared for all time.

In this lithograph from the 1860s, the artist Edward Whymper shows how one man attempted to cross a snow bridge. Many snow bridges were wider and less dangerous-looking, but clever travelers often sent their horses over first to make sure that it was safe.

THE BERGSCHRUND ON THE DENT BLANCHE IN 1865.

A Missing Woman

A partial human skeleton of a woman was found in Switzerland's Porchabella Glacier on September 1, 1988. Besides bones, police collected a brown hat, pieces of some leather shoes, a wooden bowl, and some cloth. For a time, they tried to identify the remains by checking missing person reports. When nothing matched, they stopped investigating—until Ötzi was found in 1991. Spurred by that discovery, authorities asked archaeologists to become involved, although by then four years had passed. Even so, when archaeologists arrived at the snout of the glacier, they quickly found part of a human skull that had dark-blond hair and was filled with white brain matter; they also found a preserved shoulder and left arm. Eventually, scientists determined why the police had been so unsuccessful in identifying the body. The skeleton belonged to a twenty-two-year-old woman, probably a dairymaid, who had died sometime around 1700.

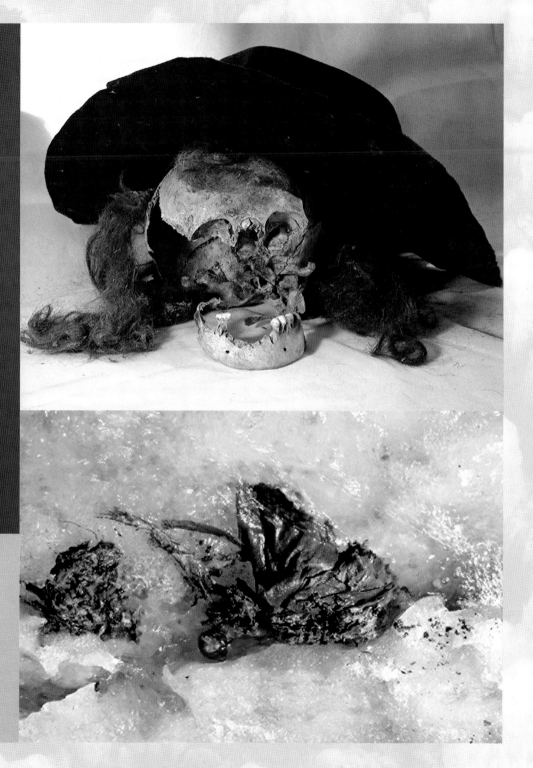

The Porchabella Glacier, which lost almost three-fourths of a mile in length in just over one hundred years, revealed the partially preserved remains of a young woman (above right). Among the over two hundred fragments recovered, bits of fabric (lower right) showed that she wore a long, lined woolen coat with wood buttons.

Often covered by a heavy veil of fog, the alpine glaciers around Chamonix frightened many people during the Little Ice Age.

CHAPTER 3

Dragons in the Ice

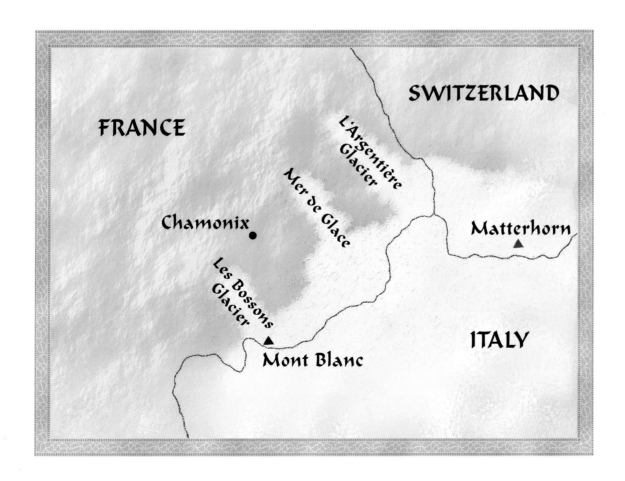

During Earth's many ice ages, glaciers stretched well beyond the polar regions into areas that are now more temperate or tropical. Even deserts such as the Sahara were covered by ice at various times.

The last ice age, scientists believe, began about thirty million years ago and ended just fifteen thousand years ago. At that time, glaciers reached their maximum coverage, blanketing almost 30 percent of the land on Earth and reaching as far south from the North Pole as New York City and St. Louis. Then, for reasons that scientists don't understand, the planet warmed and the glaciers began to retreat.

The end of an ice age, though, does not mean that glaciers disappear completely or even thaw consistently over the years. According to scientists, some twelve thousand years ago the weather cooled again for about a thousand years before the glaciers began to melt once more. Even recently, from 1500 to 1850, during what has come to be called the Little Ice Age, glaciers made a dramatic comeback, especially in North America and Europe.

During most of the Little Ice Age, people

Chamonix, nestled in the valley below, is surrounded by
some of the tallest mountains in Europe.

in Europe held strong superstitions about the nearby alpine glaciers. They considered them to be the work of the devil, created to punish sinners. They thought that dragons and other strange creatures lived there, and they believed that witches sometimes danced and cast spells there. No one wanted to visit glaciers or climb the mountains that they covered. Travelers tried to avoid them, though they sometimes had to cross a glacier for trading purposes. Even local residents who lived on the fringes were not inclined to explore them.

In fact, alpine glaciers in Europe were considered so forbidding that no one attempted to explore them until the 1700s. The first such glaciers in the world to be studied were located near Chamonix, France, at the foot of Mont Blanc, the highest mountain in Europe.

The Chamonix glaciers were so mystifying that early visitors had a difficult time describing what they looked like. In 1741, the first recorded English visitor to Chamonix wrote, "I am extremely at a loss how to give the right idea of it, as I know no one thing which I have ever seen that has the least resemblance to it." He went on to say that it resembled the icy seas of Greenland or a lake agitated "by a strong wind and frozen all at once."

Although visitors found the glaciers quite breathtaking, local residents had another reaction.

"We are terrified of the glaciers," a townsperson from Chamonix wrote in the

1600s as the glaciers advanced upon the area during the Little Ice Age. Not only were the snouts of the glaciers dangerous, but lakes from melted ice often formed within the glaciers. If the glacier shifted or melted too much, the lake could break through its icy dam and flood towns below, destroying buildings and drowning people and livestock. And avalanches caused by the buildup of glacier ice could unexpectedly cascade down the mountainside, burying everything below.

In 1642, a report mentioned that one glacier "advances by over [the length of] a musket shot every day, even in the month of August. . . . We have also heard it said that there are evil spells at work among the . . . glaciers." The same report went on to describe that a small village near Chamonix was overwhelmed by "an avalanche of snow and ice about the month of January 1642, which carried away two houses and four cows and eight sheep among which there was a girl who came to no harm although she was buried a day and a half under the snow." In 1643, another glacier near Chamonix, Les Bossons, "burst its bounds so impetuously that it carried away a third of the land" of a nearby village and caused considerable flooding and damage.

Fearing what would happen if the glaciers weren't stopped, local residents often called upon religious leaders for help. In 1644, a Catholic bishop blessed four of the "great and terrible" glaciers that surrounded towns near Chamonix. Afterward, they began to melt, retreating up the mountain. Not far away, the surging Aletsch Glacier in Switzerland threatened farms. In 1653, townspeople contacted church officials, who sent two priests to the area. After preaching to the citizens for a week, the priests led a four-hour procession of residents in the rain to the glacier where they held mass, gave a blessing, and sprinkled the snout with holy water in the name of St. Ignatius Loyola. For a while, the glacier remained still.

Eventually, despite the most sincere religious blessings, the glaciers began to advance again. In time, though, scientists came to Chamonix to see, climb, and study the glaciers. Their experiences changed people's superstitions.

One of the most famous glaciers at Chamonix is the Mer de Glace, or Icy Sea, that extends more than three miles. This postcard from about 1900 shows tourists hiking across the spectacular ice formations.

Horace de Saussure, the first scientist to climb Mont Blanc, was accompanied by a large team of guides and porters, as shown in this 1790 painting by Christian von Mechel.

A statue of Horace de Saussure and Jacques Balmat was erected in the main square of Chamonix beneath the backdrop of Mont Blanc, as shown on this souvenir booklet from the early 1900s.

The first scientist to investigate Mont Blanc was Horace de Saussure. A Swiss geologist, Saussure became interested in the rocks deposited by glaciers. On a visit to Chamonix in 1761, he saw Mont Blanc and became entranced by its majesty. Mont Blanc had never been climbed, but Saussure wanted to change that. He offered a reward to anyone who succeeded in reaching its peak; he also offered to pay the expenses of anyone who tried and failed.

Although many attempted it, the feat was not accomplished until 1786, when two men, a doctor and his guide, made the ascent. Although no one doubted that both men had reached the summit, the guide, Jacques Balmat, asserted that he had arrived well before his companion and asked to claim the reward entirely for himself. Saussure paid the reward to Balmat, but he was unhappy that neither man had studied the mountain.

As a result, Saussure climbed Mont Blanc himself—along with eighteen porters to carry the equipment and supplies. On the way, he wrote precise descriptions and took scientific measurements of everything from cloud speed to barometric pressure. At one point, he wrote, "The slope is 39 degrees, the precipice below is frightful, and the snow, hard on the surface, was flour beneath."

On the second day of Saussure's three-day ascent, one porter fell into a crevasse. Although he was not harmed, everyone realized how dangerous the climb was. "In some places," Saussure wrote in a book about the expedition, "the crevasses are quite empty;

we had to go down to the bottom and get up at the other side by stairs cut with a hatchet in the very ice and sometimes after having got to the bottom of these abysses, you can hardly conceive how you shall get out again."

When he finally reached the summit on the morning of August 2, 1787, he studied his surroundings for more than five hours in the bitterly cold temperatures. Despite the number of years and attempts it took to conquer Mont Blanc, six days after Saussure reached the summit, an Englishman named Mark Beaufoy repeated the climb, supposedly wearing nothing heavier than a pair of pajamas.

In the end, Saussure was more interested in the geology of the peaks than the glaciers themselves. But his work motivated other scientists to study glaciers: how they were

An illustrator recorded the ascent of Mont Blanc by scientist Jules-César Janssen in 1893. Unable to walk and carried by porters on a sled, Dr. Janssen was visiting an observatory named in his honor and designed by Gustave Eiffel. The wooden observatory lasted for almost thirteen years before a crevasse developed beneath it, eventually causing its collapse into the fissure.

made, how they moved, how they created moraines, why they expanded or retreated. And their work convinced people that dragons and devils did not reside in the icy landscape.

During the last half of the 1800s, tourists flocked to Chamonix, fascinated by the books written by early glacier explorers. By then, the glaciers had stopped their threatening advance, and people were intrigued to see them. Some guidebooks even recommended

A Scientific Catastrophe

In 1820, a Russian scientist named Joseph Hamel and his associates came to Chamonix hoping to perform an experiment. Dr. Hamel wondered what would happen to homing pigeons if he released them at the top of Mont Blanc—could they fly in the thinner atmosphere? Unfortunately, before the expedition reached the top, the men and their twelve mountain guides were caught in an avalanche. Three of the guides were killed, swept into a deep crevasse and covered with more than one hundred feet of snow.

After the accident, a Scottish scientist named James Forbes, who had extensively studied the speed of glaciers, estimated that the guides' bodies would emerge at the snout between thirty-eight and forty years after the accident. He was off only by one year. In 1861, forty-one years after the catastrophe, a man arrived at the local town hall carrying a cloth sack that contained objects he had retrieved from the glacier. He had found a

Le Petit Journal

SUPPLÉMENT ILLUSTRÉ

TOUS LES VENDREDIS
Le Supplément illustré
5 Centimes

Huit pages : CINQ centimes

TOUS LES JOURS
Le Petit Journal
5 Centimes

Troisième Année — SAMEDI 23 JUILLET 1892 — Numéro 87

Terrible accident dans les Alpes

A 3,800 MÈTRES D'ALTITUDE

silk-lined hat, the wing of a homing pigeon, and some well-preserved body parts: two skulls partially covered with skin and hair, a left foot, and one forearm with the hand still attached.

To verify that these were the remains of Hamel's guides, authorities quickly summoned the surviving guides, who were now quite old, and asked them to identify any of the items. One guide recognized the hat of a guide who had died and the blond-haired skull of another. Then he observed the partial arm and hand on the table.

"That . . . hand, I know it well!" he reportedly declared.

Afterward, all of the items were given to a relative of one of the dead guides; she displayed them in her home for paying tourists. Eventually, all the body parts were buried except for the foot, which was exhibited in a nearby museum.

Newspapers and magazines capitalized on the public's interest in glaciers and mountaineering by publishing often sensational illustrations of climbing accidents.

stays of twelve months in the Alps so that visitors could fully appreciate the scenery. Hotels were built on the edge of some of the glaciers, and in 1909 entrepreneurs constructed a small railroad to reach one of the largest glaciers in Europe, the Mer de Glace. Visitors toured the glaciers on horse-drawn carriages, and some hiked across the rivers of ice. Eventually, the advent of winter sports such as skiing and the rapid changes in the glaciers as they melted replaced people's fascination with the Chamonix glaciers.

Today all of Chamonix's glaciers are rapidly melting, but what remains of them gives visitors a glimpse of how amazing they once were. That vision will not last long, though, for scientists predict that most alpine glaciers in Europe will disappear by the end of this century.

Some Chamonix tourists preferred to observe the glaciers from a safe distance.

The Father of Glaciology

Hikers attempt to cross a deep crevasse on Les Bossons Glacier near Chamonix.

The father of glaciology (the study of glaciers) is Louis Agassiz, who was born and educated in Switzerland but later moved to the United States. He investigated glaciers by living on them almost year-round for five years. One of his experiments involved driving stakes in a straight line across one glacier. He realized in time that the glacier was moving forward, bending the line of the stakes into an arc.

At one point he even observed the creation of a crevasse:

I heard at a little distance a sound like the simultaneous discharge of firearms; hurrying in the direction of the noise, it was repeated under my feet with a movement like that of a slight earthquake; the ground seemed to shift and give way under me. . . . At the same time a crack opened between my feet and ran rapidly across the glacier in a straight line.

Women on the Glaciers

The first woman to climb Mont Blanc was a twenty-two-year-old servant named Marie Paradis. One day in 1808 or 1809, she encountered three mountaineers who urged her to scale the mountain with them. When they told her that tourists would want to tip her for the privilege of hearing about her adventure on Mont Blanc, she agreed to go.

Since she had never climbed a mountain before, the experience proved to be overwhelming. She summarized the experience this way: "I climbed, I could not breathe, I nearly died, they dragged me [up the last part of the mountain], carried me [to the summit], I saw black and white, and then I came down again."

As the men promised, tourists rewarded her handsomely, and she opened a small teashop with her earnings.

In 1838, a second woman made a very different ascent of Mont Blanc. An avid climber of many small mountains, Countess Henriette D'Angeville announced her desire to scale Mont Blanc. Her friends, her doctor, and even a priest tried to talk the forty-four-year-old woman out of such a foolish adventure, but she insisted.

As D'Angeville planned the ascent, she made sure that her six guides and six porters would be well fed: two legs of lamb, two ox tongues, twenty-four fowl, and six loaves of bread, among other things. For herself, she brought a small basket with writing tools, a telescope and a thermometer, some drinks, and a pocketknife. She also included a mirror because it was "a truly *feminine* article," she wrote in a book about her expedition, "which I would none the less recommend to anyone contemplating an expedition at altitude (even a captain of dragoons!). For one may use it to examine the skin to see what ravages the mountain air has wrought and remedy them by rubbing gently with cucumber pomade."

The climb over the glaciers took two days. Paintings done around that time show her in a long dress with petticoats; in truth, she changed into men's clothing for the most strenuous part of the trip. Her daring outfit included Scottish plaid wool pants lined with fleece, flannel undergarments topped with a man's shirt, a plaid coat and bonnet, and a fur-lined cloak. Her climbing outfit weighed more than twenty-one pounds.

D'Angeville reached the summit early in the afternoon of September 4, 1838. She measured the air temperature (-8 degrees centigrade), took her pulse (108 beats per minute), and wrote letters to friends and family. Next she examined the panorama through her telescope and recorded her observations in a notebook.

Then her guides said, "Now, you must go higher than Mont Blanc." Two of them locked arms, creating a seat for her, and lifted her four feet above the summit. When she returned to Chamonix, she invited sixty-year-old Marie Paradis to dine with her. Then they compared notes about their very different climbs.

Women were considered too frail to climb mountains such as Mont Blanc until Marie Paradis and Henriette D'Angeville proved them wrong.

Johan Reinhard and Miguel Zárate climbed Mount Ampato's melting glaciers to take photographs of an erupting volcano.

CHAPTER 4

Frozen Children of the Andes

High in the melting glaciers of South America's Andes Mountains, the most amazing bodies found in the ice are not accident victims but deliberate burials of centuries-old Inca children, sacrificed to appease their gods.

The children were selected for the *capacocha*, or sacrificial, ceremony apparently based on their perfect looks. A Spanish writer in 1622, Rodrigo Hernández Principe, provided an account of one child's sacrifice. Her name was Tanta Carhua, and her father, possibly a local chief, volunteered her for the honor. When her father's offer was accepted, priests escorted her from her village to the Incan capital, Cusco, where she met the emperor and participated in special festivities. Then she was led to a mountain north of

Lima, Peru, where she was sacrificed.

The capacocha ceremony on the mountains was well planned. The Inca often built rest stops, sometimes with stone buildings and other times with tents, on the way up the mountain, since the climb might take many days. At the summit, a stone platform would be ready for the ceremony. There the child would be placed inside a shaft below the platform's surface, which became a burial chamber. Sometimes a child was drugged with coca leaves or given a corn-based beer called *chicha;* then the chamber was covered with stones, and the child was left to die in the freezing temperatures. Other times, the child might be killed by strangulation or a blow to the head.

Entombed beneath the ceremonial platform, the child became an offering, perhaps to the gods who lived in the sky to prevent famine, volcanic eruptions, or even earthquakes. Later, the Inca would make pilgrimages to the burial site, where they could speak to the child and ask for help.

The anthropologist Johan Reinhard is responsible for the most dramatic discoveries of the capacocha children. His first find happened quite accidentally on Mount Ampato in Peru.

On September 8, 1995, Reinhard and his friend Miguel Zárate climbed Ampato to photograph Sabancaya, a nearby erupting volcano. The glacier that once blanketed Mount Ampato had melted dramatically in the two years prior to their climb. The ice on the ridge that led to the summit was only three feet wide, though it had been thirty feet wide a few years earlier.

As they hiked toward the summit, Zárate noticed something colorful protruding from a rocky slope. It turned out to be a small Incan statue made of gold, silver, and shell, wrapped in cloth and wearing a brightly colored feather headdress. As Zárate looked

The Prince of El Plomo

I n 1954, the first frozen Inca mummy ever discovered was found on Plomo el Cerro in Chile. Nicknamed the Prince of El Plomo, the boy was approximately eight years old and well preserved. He wore a wide silver bracelet on his right arm and was accompanied by, among other things, five small pouches that contained baby hair, baby teeth, and fingernail clippings. His face was painted red, with four yellow lines across each cheek; his hair was woven into more than two hundred tiny braids.

Scientists concluded that because of vomit found on his clothing, he had been given chicha before he was placed inside his burial tomb. The alcohol made him drowsy. He tucked his knees up under his chin, held them tightly, and froze to death.

Found by treasure hunters, the Prince of El Plomo and his grave goods were sold to the National Museum of Natural History in Santiago, Chile, where he is now exhibited.

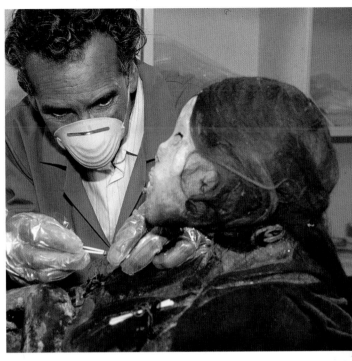

After Miguel Zárate (left) recovered the mummy bundle containing Juanita, it was delivered to scientists (above). By carefully studying the girl and her clothing, they hoped to learn more about the Inca civilization.

around, he quickly found two more.

Nearby, down the slope, the two men saw something that resembled a backpack. Later tests revealed that it was a mummy bundle, containing the well-preserved body of a fourteen-year-old girl who had died some five hundred years earlier. They realized that the body had been buried higher on the mountain, but the melting ice had weakened her burial chamber, and she had fallen down the slope. Soon named Juanita, she was the first female Incan mummy ever found.

In order to study Juanita, scientists realized that they would have to prevent her body from decomposing. This would require an expensive high-tech freezer case and a substitute unit in case the first failed. An American company offered to build the units for free if Peruvian authorities agreed to exhibit the body in the United States for a short time.

Such an offer was hard to refuse, and in May of 1996, Juanita was flown to Baltimore, Maryland. Before her exhibit at the National Geographic Society, a series of three-dimensional CT scans (a type of x-ray) were made at Johns Hopkins University. Scientists were stunned when they saw the images of her skull: instead of dying a quiet death, Juanita had been hit sharply on the right side of her head, most likely with some type of club. Her peaceful expression had been very misleading.

On the border of Chile and Argentina,
the volcano of Mount Llullaillaco was
considered sacred to the Incas.

After finding Juanita in 1995, Reinhard went on expeditions to five other Andes mountains and uncovered the bodies of fourteen sacrificed children and the grave goods that accompanied them. In March 1999, Reinhard began an expedition to the world's highest archaeological site, Mount Llullaillaco (pronounced yu-yai-YA-ko), a volcano so sacred to the Inca that they built a road to it. The ruins near its summit at twenty-two thousand feet, Reinhard suspected, might contain the body of a sacrificial victim. Climbing this peak was the ultimate test of endurance; it was also the most rewarding experience that Reinhard ever had.

The weather was terrible, and the team had to wait four days in their tents near the summit for it to clear before they could emerge. The Inca had faced the same challenges, but they had used llamas to carry building supplies so that they could construct a series of way stations. When the weather improved, Reinhard and his team found the remains of the Inca shelters, including fireplaces and grass mats, marveling at the amount of effort it would have taken the Incas to transport stones and wooden beams up the slope.

Over the next few days, they discovered 146 artifacts as well as three bundled bodies, all quickly delivered to eager researchers in the nearby town of Salta, Argentina. To their amazement, when they unwrapped the bodies, they observed three Inca children so lifelike that they seemed to be napping. In fact, of all the frozen Inca mummies ever

A stone hut built atop Mount Llullaillaco sheltered people who accompanied the children and pilgrims who visited later.

These figures, among the many artifacts found with the Llullaillaco children, were buried in this order, showing two males leading a procession of llamas. Beneath them was the bundled mummy of a boy.

found, the boy and two girls were so perfectly preserved that their hearts were filled with blood, their lungs contained air, and their brains looked as if they had died moments ago.

Researchers examined their teeth and bones to determine the children's ages and studied the goods that accompanied them.

The younger girl was six when she died. She wore a dress and a cloak and was wrapped in two blankets. Sometime after her death, her body had been struck by lightning, burning part of her head and upper abdomen. Researchers wondered if a silver plaque tied to her forehead by a cord might have served as a lightning rod. Although her face was blackened by the strike, it was otherwise undamaged. However, her head had been so deliberately and tightly wrapped in infancy that her skull was shaped like a cone, or, as the archaeologist Karen Wise wrote, "a mountain peak," indicating that she may have been raised for this sacrifice.

The boy, about seven years old, wore a red wool tunic. His face was pressed so tightly into his knees that his

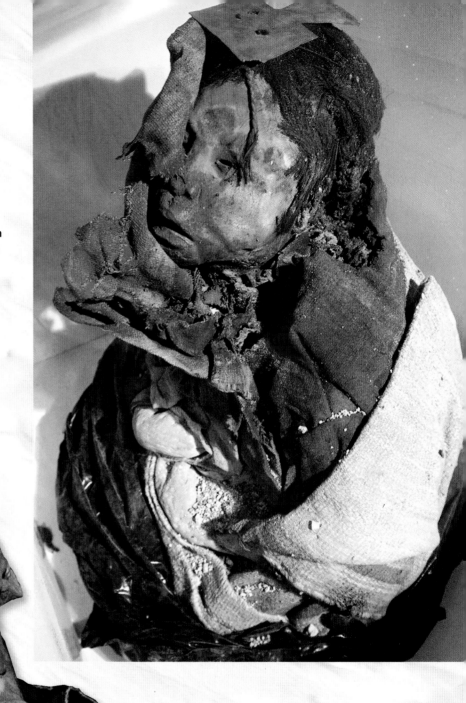

RIGHT:
A lightning strike after her burial had burned the cloth around the younger girl's head, revealing her face to surprised excavators.

BELOW:
The feet of the young boy found on Mount Llullaillaco had been bound with rope, an unusual feature for an Inca sacrifice.

nose had become flattened. Like the Prince of El Plomo, he wore a silver bracelet on his right arm. Researchers noted that his short hair, the white feather headdress that adorned his head, and his slightly deformed skull signified that he was an important member of the Inca.

The older girl, now referred to as La Doncella ("the Maiden"), was about fifteen. She wore the same type of dress as the younger girl. A man's gray tunic was found over the right part of her body; scientists wondered if someone important, perhaps her father, who might have been a chief, had asked that it accompany her as an additional offering to the god that her death celebrated. Her cheeks were tinged with red pigment and still showed indentations from her braids. Her upper lip was dusted with bits of coca leaf. Although the investigation did not reveal any signs of violent death, Reinhard wondered if the older girl had been deliberately smothered by a handful of coca leaves. One early writer, Alonso Ramos Gavilán, described in 1621 a sacrifice conducted that way.

More child sacrifices will undoubtedly be found as the glaciers of the Andes melt, but archaeologists wonder who will get there first: scientists or looters? Some Inca sites have already been plundered by grave robbers looking for valuable items such as pottery and statues that they can sell to collectors. Looters do not care about the history of the objects or the bodies they find—they are simply hoping to make money.

As a result, looters destroy the mummies while they look for items buried with them. During his four years of excavations, Reinhard even found a mummy whose head had been blown off when looters used dynamite to enter a frozen burial site. Such greed destroys the past, even as glaciers reveal more.

A study of La Doncella's hair revealed that she began eating more meat a year before death, possibly a sign that she had been selected for sacrifice at that time.

When climbers fall to their death on some mountains, recovery teams are dispatched to retrieve the body. This lithograph shows the recovery of a climber's body after an accident on Mont Blanc in about 1895.

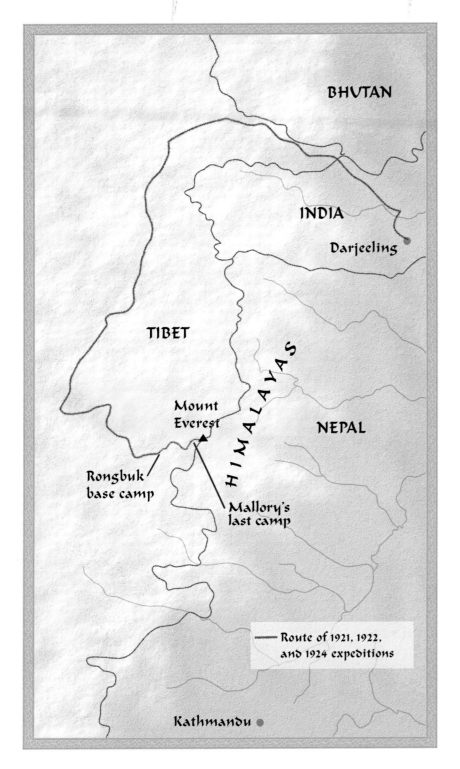

Route of 1921, 1922, and 1924 expeditions

BHUTAN

INDIA

Darjeeling

TIBET

HIMALAYAS

Mount Everest

NEPAL

Rongbuk base camp

Mallory's last camp

Kathmandu

CHAPTER 5

The Mystery of Mallory

Many climbers scaling glacier-covered mountains have died in tragic accidents. Sometimes their bodies cannot be found and recovered until decades later, when no one is able to identify the person. Although technology often helps medical examiners identify a glacier corpse today, in the past these bodies were often saved in unexpected places.

An English artist named William Brockedon occasionally visited the Alps to paint landscapes. In 1825, while staying in an inn run by Augustine monks near the Swiss-Italian border, he made a disturbing discovery. Just a few yards away was a makeshift morgue that held the remains of unidentified people who died trying to cross the glaciers high in the Alps.

The interior of the alpine morgue, complete with its unidentified corpses, that the artist William Brockeden stumbled upon was illustrated by the Swiss artist Jean DuBois in this 1837 lithograph.

He described what he found as he peered through the grated window of the morgue:

Here, the bodies of the unfortunate people who have perished in these mountains have been placed, left with their clothes on, to assist the recognition by their friends . . . just as they were found . . . and in the postures in which they have perished. Here they have "dried up and withered." . . . Upon some the clothes had remained after eighteen years,

though tattered. . . . Some of these bodies presented a hideous aspect; part of the bones of the head were exposed and blanched. . . . A mother and her child were among the latest victims; several bodies were standing against the wall . . . presenting an appalling scene.

Perhaps the most famous body of a climber ever found was discovered on the Himalayan peak of Mount Everest, the tallest mountain in the world. Once covered with snow and ice and its high valleys full of glaciers, Everest especially tantalized those in the first half of the twentieth century who hoped to climb it first. Edmund Hillary and Tenzing Norgay officially accomplished that feat in 1953. But a nagging question has overshadowed their success: Did they really reach the summit before anyone else?

The answer to this intriguing historical mystery depends on what happened on June 8, 1924, when the Englishmen George Mallory and Andrew Irvine tried to ascend Everest.

Mallory had unsuccessfully attempted to climb it in 1921 and again in 1922. When he was selected for the 1924 British Everest Expedition, some members of the 1922 expedition thought that Mallory was "quite unfit to be placed in charge of anything, including himself." A well-educated teacher and avid mountaineer, thirty-seven-year-old Mallory had little technical training in mountain climbing despite his enthusiasm for the sport. His twenty-two-year-old partner, Andrew Irvine, was an experienced climber

The Three Steps of Everest

On the day that they attempted to reach the summit of Mount Everest in 1924, George Mallory and Andrew Irvine would have taken a route over the so-called three steps. The first two steps were the most difficult: hundred-foot walls of boulders and rocks, connected by a walk along a dangerous ridge, often covered with snow. The third step was easier, some thirty feet high. Just beyond it was the pyramid-shaped summit. One question has perplexed researchers: Did they accomplish their goal?

Summit

Third Step

Second Step

First Step

Mallory's Body

Mallory's Last Camp

In 1909 the British mountaineer George Mallory climbed the Aiguille Verte, a mountain near Mont Blanc (above). Seventy-five years after he disappeared on Mount Everest, a 1999 expedition to discover the truth benefited from favorable conditions: Everest's snow cover had melted much earlier than usual that year, exposing the mountaineer's body on a windswept slope below the first step (below).

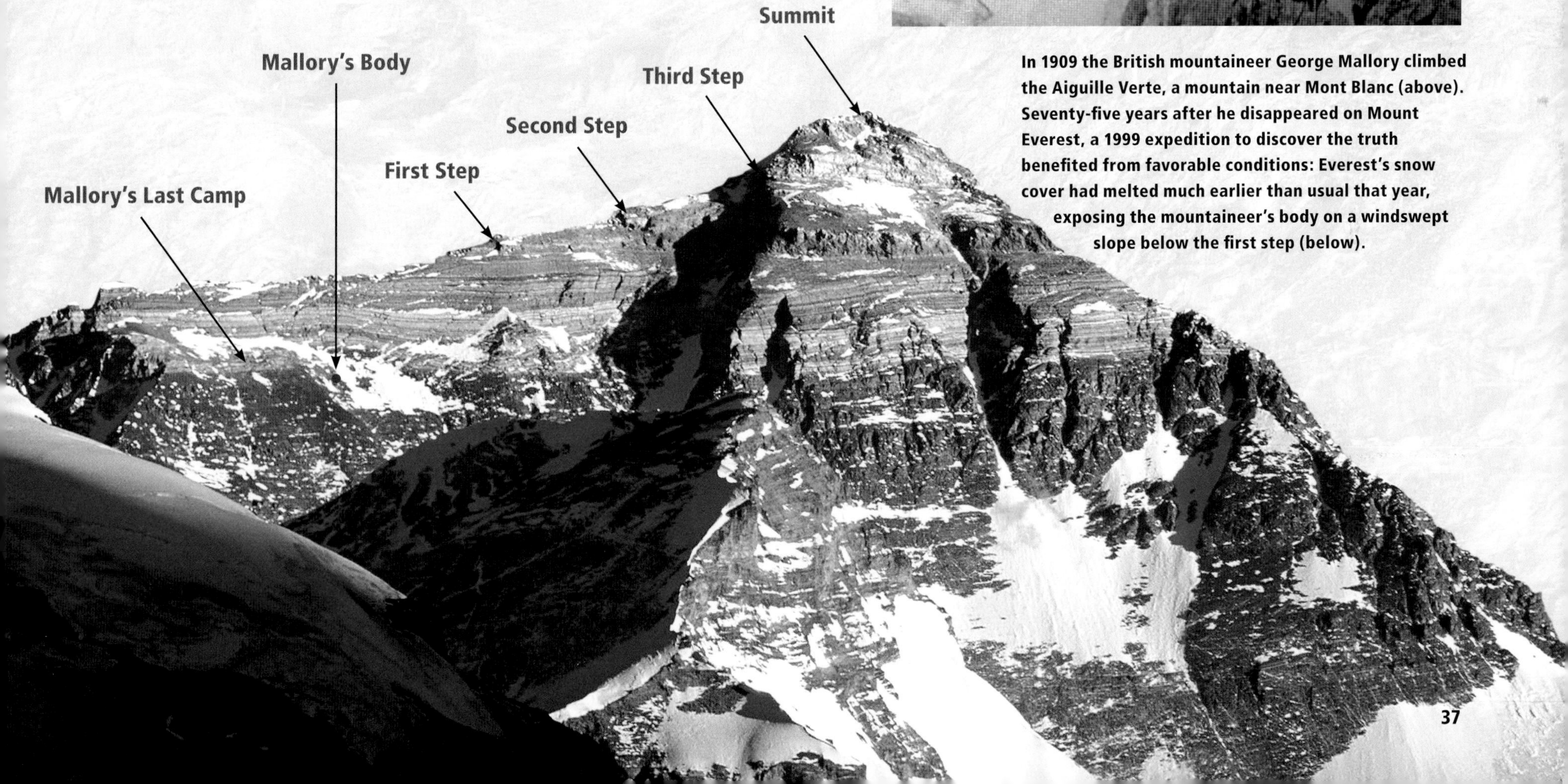

but unaccustomed to the demands of scaling a high mountain.

Early on that overcast day in 1924, Mallory and Irvine left their camp, two thousand feet beneath the summit, alone. The air was so thin at that altitude that Mallory had arranged to take oxygen cylinders to help them breathe as they made their way over the three steps to the summit. At sea level, the climb would have been strenuous enough, but in the oxygen-deprived atmosphere it would be monumentally difficult and very time-consuming.

That afternoon at about one, another member of the expedition, Noel Odell, faced the cloud-covered peak, just as the weather momentarily improved. He later wrote:

> There was a sudden clearing of the atmosphere, and the entire summit ridge and final peak of Everest were unveiled. My eyes became fixed on one tiny black spot silhouetted on a small snow-crest beneath a rock-step in the ridge; the black spot moved. Another black spot became apparent and moved up the snow to join the other on the crest.

Convinced that the tiny specks were Mallory and Irvine climbing the second step, Odell was quite concerned. The men were still three hours away from reaching the summit and well behind schedule. He knew that if they kept going, they would be descending to the camp in deadly darkness.

His concern was justified, for they never returned, and members of their expedition were unable to search for their bodies. Even if they had located them, transporting them down Everest would have been too dangerous a task.

Many people wondered not only what happened to the men, but also whether they reached the summit that day. Over the years, the mystery has deepened. In 1933, another expedition found Irvine's ice ax below the first step; researchers wondered if it had fallen or been placed there deliberately. In 1979, a Chinese mountaineer claimed to have seen a "dead Englishman" near the location of Mallory's last camp. But before he could give more details, he was killed in an avalanche. In 1991, another mountaineer stumbled across an antique oxygen canister beneath the first step; he wondered if Mallory and Irvine had left it there.

In 1999, a new expedition was organized. Team members hoped to locate the body found by the Chinese climber and discover what had happened.

The expedition found that after seventy-five years, the terrain around Mount Everest had changed quite a bit. Glaciers that had been wide on the way up Mount Everest had shrunk, and snow and ice patches near the summit had thinned considerably.

After selecting a specific area to search for the body, the team fanned out on a barren windy slope. Soon they found a man's frozen body lying face-down beneath the summit.

Most likely buried in snow and ice at various points during the last seventy-five years, the corpse had been uncovered in recent years, long enough that the clothing on the back had disintegrated and the exposed skin had been bleached white by the sun. However, his hands, clutching the small rocks on the side of the slope as if to help stop his final downward slide, were much darker in color and had perhaps been covered

Mallory's left leg seemed to cover his injured right leg; his hobnail boot probably came off in the fall.

Expedition members were surprised that they had found the body of George Mallory, not Andrew Irvine.

Mallory's snow goggles were in his pocket, possibly indicating that he had reached the summit and was descending the mountain at night.

Mallory and Irvine's accident on Mount Everest may have resembled this one illustrated in an 1894 newspaper. Two men anxious to climb the Matterhorn made an error in judgment and fell to their deaths. In the case of Mallory and Irvine, the rope connecting the men would have snapped. No one knows who fell first or where Irvine's body lies.

longer. His right leg was twisted, broken badly in the fall that ended his life.

At first, the team believed they had found Irvine, since the body was below the area where the ice pick had been found. But team members inspected the clothing, they discovered a laundry tag sewn onto a shirt: G. Mallory. They had found Mallory instead of Irvine.

Once they had pried the frozen body from the slope, they searched it for possessions. They found goggles tucked into one pocket. They also located canned food, an altimeter, a monogrammed handkerchief, and some letters. They checked in vain for a photo that Mallory was said to have carried. According to his daughter, Mallory had told his family that he would leave a photograph of his wife at the summit as a memento of his accomplishment.

Unable to carry Mallory's body safely down the mountain, the team buried it under rocks before they left.

Afterward, team members disagreed about the meaning of the discovery. Some concluded that Mallory had reached the top of Mount Everest on the day that he died. They pointed out that he was not carrying the photograph of his wife as proof that he had reached the summit. The snow goggles they had found in his pocket also proved that he had reached the top and was climbing down the mountain in darkness.

Others were skeptical. One team member, Conrad Anker, even went so far as to try to climb the second step himself. Today, most mountaineers

who climb the second step use a ladder left behind by other climbers in 1975. But no such ladder existed in 1924, and Mallory would have had to climb that section without any help. When Anker attempted the second step without the ladder, he failed, convincing him that Mallory had not made it to the summit in 1924. In 2007, though, Anker made another attempt. This time, he reached the top of the second step without the ladder and changed his mind. "What I have learned," he wrote on his blog, "is that Mallory and Irvine could have climbed it, and that is worth thinking about."

What both sides agreed on, however, was that Mallory and Irvine were roped together before their lives ended. A rope was still tied around Mallory's waist when his body was discovered. Because his body had not suffered terrible injuries, members of the 1999 expedition concluded that he had not fallen from a great height, but that the rope connecting him to Irvine had snapped during the fall.

Today about fifty teams attempt to climb the mountain each year, some of them looking for the remains of Andrew Irvine to solve the final mystery of who reached Everest's summit first.

The government of Nepal, hoping to discourage casual tourists, charges climbing teams approximately $100,000, but sterner measures may be enforced soon. As Everest's glaciers melt, as its snow- and ice-covered peak thaws, and as climbing debris—including some 188 corpses of fallen and unrecovered climbers—accumulates on its slopes, some conservationists have called for the popular mountain to be closed to mountaineers.

Should that happen, the mystery will remain unsolved forever.

In these photos of Mount Everest, the melting of the glaciers below and near the summit of Mount Everest is quite visible. The top photo is from 1968; the bottom from 2007.

St. Elias Mountains

CANADA

YUKON

•Whitehorse

UNITED
STATES

Site of
discovery
Tatshenshini-
Alsek Park

BRITISH COLUMBIA

Haines•

Pacific
Ocean

ALASKA   Gustavus•   Juneau
•

A well-preserved but
partial body of a man was
excavated on the edge of a
melting Canadian glacier.

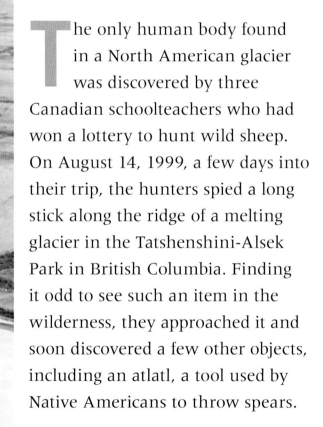

CHAPTER 6

Another Man from a Glacier

The only human body found in a North American glacier was discovered by three Canadian schoolteachers who had won a lottery to hunt wild sheep. On August 14, 1999, a few days into their trip, the hunters spied a long stick along the ridge of a melting glacier in the Tatshenshini-Alsek Park in British Columbia. Finding it odd to see such an item in the wilderness, they approached it and soon discovered a few other objects, including an atlatl, a tool used by Native Americans to throw spears.

Then they saw the body.

"There was a big smear on the snow," Bill Hanlon, one of the hunters, told reporters. "It looked like an animal had died. . . . I looked about three feet away and there was a pelvic

In order to transport the body, excavators carefully wrapped it; no photographs of the body itself were ever taken.

bone sticking up from the ice. I could see legs going down into the ice. . . . I knew we had stumbled onto something big."

The men didn't touch the body but they did place the other artifacts in a plastic bag in preparation for their long hike back to civilization. Three days later, they reported their find to officials at a museum in Whitehorse, Canada, hoping that someone would be able to solve the mystery.

The body and its related artifacts were removed from the ice over a two-day period. Scientists examined the remains at the Royal BC Museum in Victoria, Canada. The body, which turned out to be a man, was fairly well preserved in two parts. The headless abdomen was missing the right arm; the separate lower body was missing the right leg beneath the knee. Goose bumps still covered the skin. Although the man's head was missing, his long black unbraided hair was found alongside the body. They concluded that he was about twenty years old because certain parts of his collarbone and spine had not yet fused.

Researchers studied the objects that accompanied him: his woven spruce root hat with a broad brim, his squirrel fur robe, his knife in a leather sheath, and his leather food pouch that held pieces of salmon. A walking stick and an atlatl, also found nearby, probably did not belong to him.

At first, scientists thought that they might have found another ancient man such as Ötzi. But radiocarbon testing revealed that the young man had died sometime between 1670 and 1850. Because he was found on

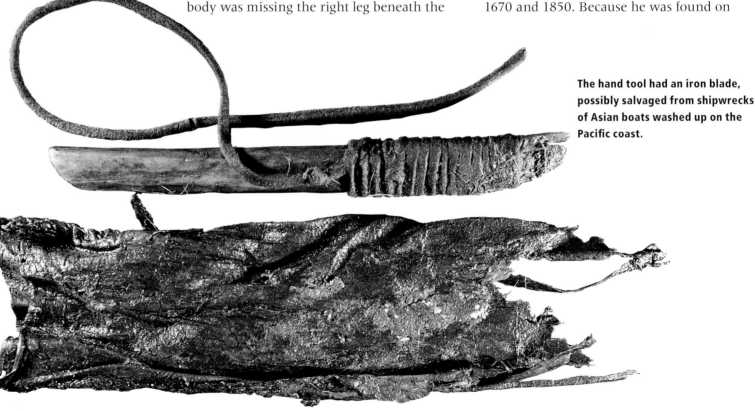

The hand tool had an iron blade, possibly salvaged from shipwrecks of Asian boats washed up on the Pacific coast.

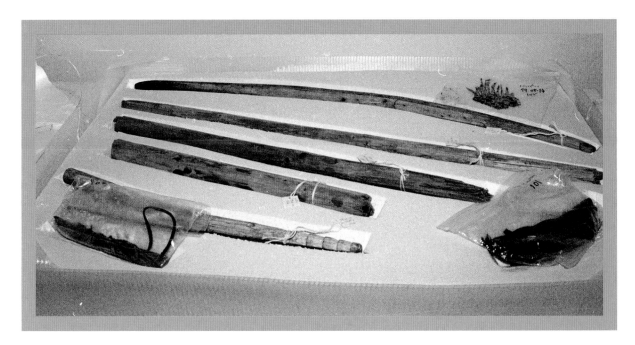

One mystery about Kwäday Dan Ts'ìnchí is that some of the wooden artifacts found near his body are not as old as the body and clothing.

the land of the Champagne and Aishihik First Nations, members thought that the man might be a distant relative. In fact, First Nations storytellers told many folktales about a traveler from the coastal area who fell into a crevasse on his way home from a trip inland. They also related many stories about the glaciers on their lands.

They agreed to allow the study of the remains as long as they were returned to the nation. Because he was found on their territory and was considered their responsibility, the First Nations named him Kwäday Dan Ts'ìnchí (or "Long Ago Person Found" in the Southern Tutchone language).

During the months that followed, scientists performed various tests on Kwäday Dan Ts'ìnchí to understand his lifestyle. By examining his stomach and large intestine,

scientists discovered that in the three days before he died he had eaten beach asparagus and had drunk melted glacier ice. He may also have consumed some type of meat, salmon, and some berries. By studying the pollen in his intestine and on his clothing, scientists concluded that in the last few days before he died, Kwäday Dan Ts'ìnchí had traveled quite a bit, through different elevations and different landscapes. The type and amount of pollen also indicated that he had probably died in either late July or August, when a certain plant, *Salicornia*, was in bloom. They could not decide, however, exactly where he was from, though they suspected that he had spent some time on or near the Pacific coast for most of his life before he moved farther inland.

They also wondered how he died. At first, researchers believed that the man had fallen

The Past, Alive

Could Kwäday Dan Ts'ìnchí be related to any living members of the First Nations? To find out, scientists compared DNA samples from 248 First Nations volunteers to the DNA of the Long Ago Person Found. The amazing results revealed that seventeen participants were related to Kwäday Dan Ts'ìnchí, meaning they had a common female ancestor – perhaps a grandmother, mother, sister, or another close relative of Long Ago Person Found. Such clear connections between the past and present are very unusual in archaeology.

The scientists Kjerstin Mackie and Valerie Thorp at the Royal BC Museum examine the squirrel fur garment worn by Kwäday Dan Ts'ìnchí.

into a crevasse, but later analysis suggested that he might have simply sat down to rest and died in a midsummer snowstorm. After all, they reasoned, he lived during the time of the Little Ice Age, when the weather was much colder and less predictable. A summer snowstorm would not have been impossible then. A heavy snowfall would have covered his body, preserving it, as the glacier accumulated around him. When the ice shifted sometime later, he was torn into pieces.

In July 2001, the remains of Kwäday Dan Ts'ìnchí were cremated and returned to the tribe for a potlatch, or funeral, planned by aboriginal community members from both interior and coastal areas. Afterward, a handful of people accompanied the remains to the discovery site, where his ashes were buried. All of the artifacts, except a small pouch, were saved, but they are not displayed anywhere.

Then something just as extraordinary happened.

In August 2003, two of the sheep hunters returned to the park to hunt as well as pay their respects at a rock monument built near the discovery site by members of the First Nations to honor Kwäday Dan Ts'ìnchí. The glacier had melted considerably since 1999, and as they approached the monument, they were stunned to see pieces of skull on the surface of the thawing ice. When authorities investigated the site that summer and the next, they also found some finger bones and

The father of this Tlingit family, pictured near Dyea, Alaska, about 1895, wears an everyday woven spruce root hat similar to the one found with Kwäday Dan Ts'ìnchí.

a wooden artifact. They examined the items on the receding glacier. Then they left the bones forever in the area where Kwäday Dan Ts'ìnchí had lost his life.

In the past ten years, the melting glaciers of North America have released many other items, including a 1,400-year-old moccasin from the southwestern part of Canada's Yukon province and a 340-year-old bison skull from Colorado's 13,000-foot-high Continental Divide, an unusually high location for a bison to be found.

Archaeologists are so concerned about the rapid melting of North American glaciers that they are trying not to leave future discoveries only to chance. In fact, they sometimes use helicopters to search for small patches of melting ice that allow for quick excavation.

So far, no other frozen human remains have been discovered in North America, but that may change as glaciers continue to melt.

More discoveries from the past may be made as the glaciers along the Continental Divide thaw. This is a retreating cirque glacier at the Rocky Mountain National Park in Colorado.

One of the few remaining glaciers on the African continent is at the top of Mount Kilimanjaro. Scientists predict that it will disappear in fifty years or less.

CHAPTER 7

Saving the Past

As more bodies and artifacts from the past appear at the edges of melting alpine glaciers, they may be preserved if they are found soon after they resurface.

But such remarkable discoveries have a high price. Himalayan glaciers are said to be retreating faster than any others—more than 2,000 of its 160,000 glaciers have disappeared in the last century. In Africa, the few glaciers that remain are shrinking so fast that some scientists predict they will

Glaciers now cover only about 10 percent of the earth's surface, an amount that has been declining each year.

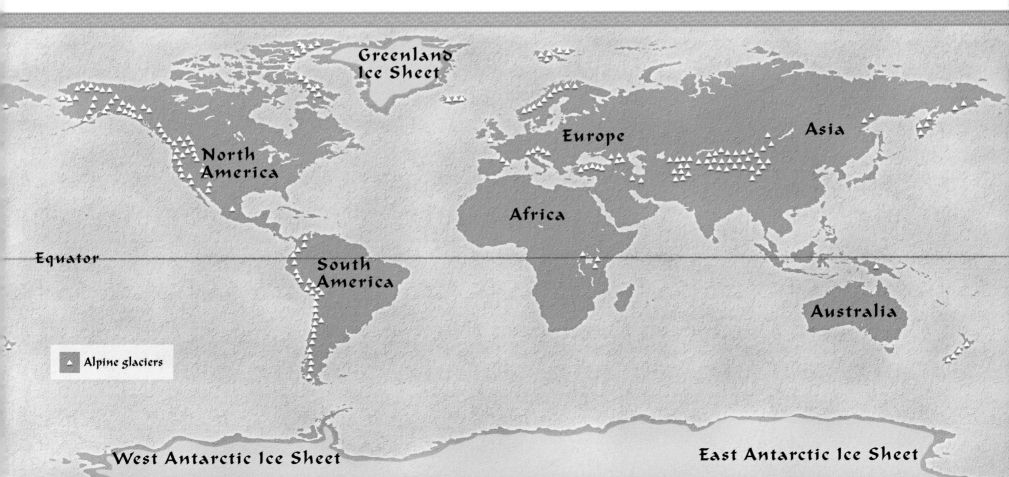

Greenland Ice Sheet

Europe

Asia

North America

Africa

Equator

South America

Australia

▲ Alpine glaciers

West Antarctic Ice Sheet

East Antarctic Ice Sheet

This rushing stream in northwest Pakistan is fed by Himalayan glaciers. If they disappear as predicted in forty to fifty years, the main source of water for Pakistan will be gone, causing severe water shortages.

completely disappear in twenty to fifty years. The smallest South American glaciers, one glaciologist calculates, will disappear within the next fifteen years; they comprise about 80 percent of the total glaciers on the continent. In the United States, Montana's renowned Glacier National Park, which once had 150 glaciers a century ago, has lost all but a few dozen; scientists expect that those will be gone in the next fifty years.

As glaciers disappear, greater problems await. Because they provide the largest share of the Earth's fresh drinking water, glaciers that thaw completely can no longer feed rivers or streams. As a result, serious long-term droughts are likely to occur. Glaciers in the Himalayas supply water for the Ganges Basin, one of the longest river systems where one-tenth of the Earth's population lives. If these glaciers substantially recede, a large portion of the Ganges' water supply will simply dry up. Similarly, if glaciers in the Andes disappear, countries that border the mountain chain will have severely reduced water supplies. For example, Ecuador's capital city, Quito, gets half of its water from a nearby glacier. Once that glacier evaporates, Quito will have to find half of its water elsewhere.

Of even greater concern to glaciologists is what will happen to Antarctica, which contains three of the five largest glacial ice sheets on Earth (the small Antarctic Peninsula, the West Antarctic, and the massive East Antarctic ice sheets), as well as 85 percent of the world's fresh, but frozen, surface water. Because melting Antarctic

A ski resort on Switzerland's Tortin Glacier uses an insulated cover to reflect the sun and slow further melting. Such attempts are only temporary measures at best. Some entrepreneurs want to build a four-hundred-foot-tall pressurized restaurant and conference center on the top of Switzerland's Little Matterhorn, to keep tourists coming to the Alps even if the snow disappears.

glaciers would fill the ocean with more water, sea levels would rise, flooding low-lying areas around the world. Already many glaciers on the Antarctic Peninsula have shown considerable retreat. Now glaciologists wonder if the West and East Antarctic ice sheets will follow the same pattern.

Although no one knows for certain what will happen, scientists remain very concerned. They wonder why glaciers have melted so rapidly in recent years and if there are steps that can help stop the retreat. Some have asked if humans and the pollution they create are responsible for the dramatic meltdown. Others have questioned if the melting is simply a result of a normal ice age cycle on Earth that has occurred a number of times over the past 4.6 billion years. Or, could a combination of the two explain the dramatic loss of glaciers around the world?

The only way to know for certain would be to travel in a time machine to a future time some twenty-five thousand or fifty thousand years from now, when some scientists believe another ice age cycle might begin. The time traveler would be able to observe the answer. If she sees a dry and perhaps desolate Earth, pollution may have irreparably caused glaciers to melt and the Earth to warm. If she sees advancing glaciers, a naturally occurring

These photos of Chamonix's Mer de Glace taken about one hundred years apart show how much it has melted. The glacier is now quite shallow, and many of its unique formations are gone.

ice age cycle may have temporarily caused glaciers to retreat before they surged again.

Sadly, there is no way to know the answer now. Governments and their policies may provide the most important key, but it is up to each individual to make a personal decision about global warming and act accordingly. If you want to change the effect that you have on the planet, the best place to start is in your own home.

In the meantime, visit an alpine glacier while you can. If glaciers continue to melt, you may never get another chance.

Visitors to Switzerland's Rhone Glacier in the early part of the twentieth century were escorted in open-air touring cars shown in this souvenir postcard.

Personal Ways to Help the Environment

USE LESS ENERGY.
- Replace regular light bulbs with compact fluorescent bulbs; adjust your thermostat (higher in summer, lower in winter); turn off lights and other electrical items when not in use; replace inefficient appliances; use a manual lawnmower; buy locally produced products and foodstuffs (which require minimal transportation to reach you).

PRODUCE LESS WASTE.
- Bring reusable bags to the grocery store; buy recycled paper; recycle your garbage; avoid buying over-packaged products; use less water (by turning on the dishwasher and washing machine only when full, using a low-flow showerhead, and taking shorter showers).

MONITOR YOUR TRANSPORTATION.
- Maintain your family car (keep the tires properly inflated; clean and change filters regularly); buy a fuel-efficient or hybrid car; walk or ride a bike whenever possible.

PLANT TREES.
- Trees filter carbon dioxide from the air.

STAY INFORMED.
- Read the news daily to learn more about what is happening to the environment and how you can help.

Glaciers to Visit

Argentina

Los Glaciares National Park

Austria

Pasterze Glacier

Canada

Columbia Icefield
(including the Athabasca
Glacier), Alberta

Chile

Bernardo O'Higgins
National Park (including
Pio XI Glacier)

Torres del Paine National Park
(including Grey Glacier)

Ecuador

Cotopaxi Glacier, Ecuador

France

Mer de Glace and Les Bossons
Glacier (and others)

Germany

Zugspitze Glacier

Iceland

Vatnajökull Glacier

New Zealand

Fox Glacier and Franz
Josef Glacier

Norway

Jostedalsbreen National
Park and Glacier

Switzerland

Glacier Express (train from
St. Moritz to Zermatt)

Rhône Glacier

United States

Carbon Glacier,
Washington

Glacier Bay National Park,
Alaska

Glacier National Park,
Montana

Mendenhall Glacier,
Alaska

Palmer Glacier, Oregon

St. Mary's Glacier,
Colorado

Suggested Websites

GLACIERS

All About Glaciers: http://nsidc.org/glaciers/

The Glacier Archive (in German): www.gletscherarchiv.de/

Glaciers Online: www.swisseduc.ch/glaciers/index-en.html

Swiss Glacier Monitoring Network:
http://glaciology.ethz.ch/messnetz/index.html

The Canary Project: Glacial, Icecap, and Permafrost Melting:
www.canary-project.org/photos_pasterze_austria.html

High Altitude Scientific and Technological Research:
www.evk2cnr.org/en/

Glacier Page: www.jamesmdeem.com/page.glacier.htm

ÖTZI THE ICEMAN

South Tyrol Museum of Archaeology: www.iceman.it

The Mummy Tombs: www.mummytomb.com/otzi.htm

INCA DISCOVERIES

Johan Reinhard's Journeys: www.mountain.org/reinhard/

Museum of High Altitude Archaeology, Salta, Argentina:
www.maam.org.ar

Museo Santuarios de Altura in Arequipa, Peru:
www.ucsm.edu.pe/santury/

GEORGE MALLORY

Everest News: www.everestnews.com/Default.htm

KWÄDAY DAN TS'ÌNCHÍ
Kwäday Dan Ts'ìnchí Archaeology:
www.tsa.gov.bc.ca/archaeology/kwaday_d%C3%A4n_
ts%E2%80%99inchi/index.htm

Acknowledgments and Bibliography

Researching and writing this book has been a long and thoughtful expedition to uncover the truth about glaciers. In my journeys to these fascinating and unusual places, many people aided me in my quest to find information and photographs. In particular, I would like to thank:

—Marco Samadelli of the South Tyrol Archaeology Museum in Bolzano, Italy

—Peter Graf of the Matterhorn Museum in Zermatt, Switzerland

—Sheila Greer of the Champagne and Aishihik First Nations, Canada

—Michael Hambrey and Juerg Alean, professors of glaciology

—Marcel Guntert, director of the Natural History Museum in Bern, Switzerland

—Johan Reinhard, anthropologist and explorer

—Kjerstin Mackie of the Royal BC Museum in Victoria, British Columbia, Canada

Agassiz, Elizabeth Cabot Cary. *Louis Agassiz: His Life and Correspondence.* Vol. 1. Boston: Houghton Mifflin, 1885.

Anker, Conrad, and David Roberts. *The Lost Explorer: Finding Mallory on Mount Everest.* New York: Simon and Shuster, 1999.

Ardito, Stefano. *Mont Blanc.* Vercelli, Italy: White Star, 2006.

Aufderheide, Arthur C. *The Scientific Study of Mummies.* Cambridge, UK: Cambridge University Press, 2003.

Ballu, Yves. *A la Conquête de Mont Blanc.* Paris: Gallimard, 1986.

Baroni, Carlo. "The Alpine 'Iceman' and Holocene Climate Change." *Quaternanry Research* 46 (1996): 78–83.

Bates, Robert H. *Mystery, Beauty, and Danger: The Literature of the Mountains and Mountain Climbing Published in England Before 1946.* Portsmouth, NH: Peter E. Randall, 2001.

Benn, Douglas I., and David J. A. Evans. *Glaciers and Glaciation.* London: Arnold, 2006.

Bowen, Mark. *Thin Ice: Unlocking the Secrets of Climate in the World's Highest Mountains.* New York: Henry Holt, 2005.

Brockedon, William. *Journals of Excursions in the Alps.* London: James Duncan, 1833.

Brown, Rebecca A. *Women on High: Pioneers of Mountaineering.* Boston: Appalachian Mountain Club Books, 2002.

Cruikshank, Julie. *Do Glaciers Listen? Local Knowledge, Colonial Encounters, and Social Imagination.* Vancouver: University of British Columbia Press, 2005.

Cullen, Bob. "Testimony from the Iceman." *Smithsonian* (Feb. 2003): 42–49.

D'Angeville, Henriette. *My Ascent of Mont Blanc.* Translated by Jennifer Barnes. London: HarperCollins, 1992.

Dickson, James H., et al. "Kwäday Dan Ts'ìnchí, the First Ancient Body of a Man from a North American Glacier: Reconstructing His Last Days by Intestinal and Biomolecular Analyses." *Holocene* 14, no. 4 (2004): 481–86.

Dickson, James H., Klaus Oeggl, and Linda L. Handley. "The Iceman Reconsidered." *Scientific American* (May 2003): 4–13.

Dixon, E. James, William F. Manley, and Craig M. Lee. "The Emerging Archaeology of Glaciers and Ice Patches: Examples from Alaska's Wrangell-St. Elias National Park and Preserve." *American Antiquity* 70 (Jan. 2005): 129–44.

"DNA Testing May Offer Clues About Man in Ice; Melt Led to Discovery of 550-Year-Old Remains." *Washington Post,* June 6, 2002, A20.

Fagan, Brian. *The Little Ice Age: How Climate Made History 1300–1850.* New York: Basic Books, 2000.

Fleckinger, Angela. *Ötzi, the Iceman.* Second edition. Vienna, Austria: Folio, 2005.

Fleming, Fergus. *Killing Dragons: The Conquest of the Alps.* New York: Grove Press, 2000.

————. *Off the Map: Tales of Endurance and Exploration*. New York: Grove Press, 2004.

Fowler, Brenda. "Following Stone Age Footsteps." *New York Times,* August 3, 1997, sec. 5, p. 13.

————. *Iceman: Uncovering the Life and Times of a Prehistoric Man Found in an Alpine Glacier*. New York: Random House, 2000.

Grove, Jean M. "The Little Ice Age in the Massif of Mont Blanc." *Transactions, Institute of British Geographers* (Dec. 1966): 129–43.

Guyton, Bill. *Glaciers of California: Modern Glaciers, Ice Age Glaciers, the Origin of Yosemite Valley, and a Glacier Tour in the Sierra Nevada*. Berkeley: University of California Press, 1998.

Hambrey, Michael, and Jürg Alean. *Glaciers.* 2nd edition. Cambridge, UK: Cambridge University Press, 2004.

Hemmleb, Jochen, Larry A. Johnson, and Eric R. Simonson. *Ghosts of Everest: The Search for Mallory and Irvine*. Seattle: Mountaineers Books, 1999.

Horne, P. D. "The Prince of El Plomo: A Frozen Treasure." In Konrad Spindler et al. (eds.), *Human Mummies: A Global Survey of Their Status and the Techniques of Conservation*. Vienna, Austria: Springer, 1996.

Jones, Jonathan. "Into the White." *Guardian,* Dec. 18, 2006, 23.

Krajick, Kevin. "Melting Glaciers Release Ancient Relics." *Science* (April 19, 2002): 454–56.

Lehner, Peter, and Annemarie Julen. "A Man's Bones with 16th Century Weapons and Coins in a Glacier near Zermatt, Switzerland." *Antiquity* 65 (1991): 269–73.

Le Roy Ladurie, Emmanuel. *Times of Feast, Times of Famine: A History of Climate Since the Year 1000.* Translated by Barbara Bray. Garden City, NY: Doubleday, 1971.

McDougall, Dan. "Should Everest Be Closed?" *Observer,* Oct. 8, 2006, 8.

Macdougall, Doug. *Frozen Earth: The Once and Future Story of Ice Ages*. Berkeley: University of California Press, 2004.

Markels, Alex. "Defrosting the Past." *U.S. News & World Report*, Sept. 16, 2002, 63–64.

————. "See a Glacier (Before It Melts)." *U.S. News & World Report*, Dec. 25, 2006, 88.

Mazel, David (ed.). *Mountaineering Women: Stories by Early Climbers*. College Station: Texas A&M University Press, 1994.

Pringle, Heather. *The Mummy Congress: Science, Obsession, and the Everlasting Dead*. New York: Hyperion, 2001.

————. "Out of the ice: Who was the ancient traveler discovered in an alpine glacier?" *Canadian Geographic* (July/Aug. 2002): 56–64.

————. "Unlocking the Secrets of the Iceman." *Canadian Geographic* (Nov./Dec. 1999): 19.

Reid, Howard. *In Search of the Immortals: Mummies, Death, and the Afterlife*. New York: St. Martin's Press, 2001.

Reinhard, Johan. "At 22,000 Feet Children of Inca Sacrifice Found Frozen in Time." *National Geographic* (Nov. 1999): 36–55.

————. *The Ice Maiden: Inca Mummies, Mountain Gods, and Sacred Sites in the Andes.* Washington, D.C.: National Geographic, 2005.

————. "Peru's Ice Maidens: Unwrapping the Secrets." *National Geographic* (June 1996): 62–81.

————. "Sharp Eyes of Science Probe the Mummies of Peru." *National Geographic* (Jan. 1997): 36–43.

Schobinger, Juan. "Sacrifices of the High Andes." *Natural History* (April 1991): 62–68.

Spindler, Konrad. *The Man in the Ice*. London: Weidenfeld and Nicolson, 1994.

Stadler, Harald. "Subordinate versus Superior: The Glacier Corpse of the Poacher Norbert Mattersberger Found on the Gradetzkees in the East Tyrol." www.uibk.ac.at/urgeschichte/harald.stadler/subordinate_versus_superior.html.

Twain, Mark. *A Tramp Abroad*. New York: Harper & Brothers, 1907.

Ueverest: The Altitude Everest Expedition 2007. www.ueverest.com/

Wise, Karen. "High Mountain Inca Sacrifices." In Paul Bahn (ed.), *Written in Bones: How Human Remains Unlock the Secrets of the Dead*. Newton Abbot, UK: David and Charles, 2002.

Illustration Credits

Index

Page numbers in *italics* refer to illustrations.

A

Agassiz, Louis, 24
Andes Mountains, *27*
   Inca children, 27–33, *28, 29, 32, 33*
   melting of the glaciers, 51
   Mount Ampato, *26,* 28
   Mount Llullaillaco, *30, 31,* 31–33
Anker, Conrad, 40, 41
Antarctica, 51–52
avalanches, 20, 22, 38

B

Balmat, Jacques, 21, *21,* 23
Beaufoy, Mark, 22
British Everest Expedition of 1924,
   36, 38–41
Brockedon, William, 35–36
Canada
   Axel Heilberg Island, *12*
   British Columbia, *42,* 43–47
   Yukon, 47

C

Champagne-Aishihik First Nations, 45,
   46, *46*
Chile, Plomo el Cerro, 28
Colorado, 47, *47*

D

D'Angeville, Henriette, 25
de Saussure, Horace, 21, *21*

E

environment, ways to help, 53

F

figurines, Inca, *31*
Forbes, James, 22–23
France, Chamonix Valley, *16,* 17–25, *52*

G

glaciers
   advancement, 12, 20, 22, 24
   Aletsch, 20
   of Chamonix Valley, *16,* 17–25, *52*
   characteristics, 11, *11*
   Crusoe, *12*
   early research, 19–22, *21, 22, 24, 24*
   formation, 11
   Glärnisch, *11*
   Les Bossons, 20, *24*
   Madatsch, 12
   melting (*See* melting of the glaciers)
   Mer de Glace, 20, 24, *52*
   Mount Kilimanjaro, *48*
   Niederjoch, *1,* 1–2, *3, 5, 10*
   Porchabella, 15
   superstitions, 19, 20
   Tatshenshini-Alsek, *42,* 43–47
   Theodul, *9, 13,* 13–14
   types, 10
global warming, 49–53

H

hair
   Inca children, 28, *28, 29, 32,* 33
   Kwäday Dan Ts'ìnchí, 44
   Porchabella Glacier woman, *15*
Hamel, Joseph, 22–23
Hanlon, Bill, 43
hats, 5, *15,* 23, 33, 44, *46*
Hillary, Edmund, 36

I

Incas, sacrificial children, 27–33,
   28, 29, 32, 33
Irvine, Andrew, 36–41, *40*
Italy
   Niederjoch Glacier, *1,* 1–2, *3, 5, 10*
   Theodul Glacier, *9, 13,* 13–14

J

Janssen, Jules-César, *22*
jewelry, *28, 33*
Juanita, 29, *29, 31*

K

Kwäday Dan Ts'ìnchí, *42,* 43–47

L

La Doncella, 33, *33*
Little Ice Age, *16,* 17, 19, 20, 46
looters, 6, 28, 33

M

Mackie, Kjerstin, *46*
Mallory, George, 36–41, *38, 39, 40*
melting of the glaciers
   Alps, 1, 24, *51*
   Andes, 51
   global warming, 49–53
   Mount Everest and Himalayas, *37,*
     38, *41,* 41, 49, *50,* 51
   Mount Kilimanjaro and Africa,
     48, 49
   Rocky Mountains, 47–48, 51
   South America, 49, 51
Montana, 51
Mont Blanc, 19, *21,* 21–22, *22, 24,* 25, *25*
Mont Blanc Expedition of 1820,
   22–23, *23*
morgue, alpine, 36, *36*
mountain climbers
   British Everest Expeditions, 36,
     38–41
   Mont Blanc, 25, *25, 34*
   women, 25, *25*
Mount Everest, 35, 36–41, *37, 39, 41*
Mount Kilimanjaro, *48*
Mount Llullaillaco, *30, 31,* 31–33
mummification process, 10

N

Nepal, 41
Niederjoch Glacier man. *See* Ötzi
Norgay, Tenzing, 36

O

Odell, Noel, 38
Ötzi
   autopsy results, 4, *4,* 6, 7, 9–10
   death of, 7
   discovery, 1–4, *2, 6,* 12
   excavation, *3,* 4, *5, 6,* 7
   preservation conditions, 10, 12, 14
   tattoos, *4*

P

Pakistan, *50*
Paradis, Marie, 25, *25*
Porchabella Glacier woman, 15, *15*
Prince of El Plomo, 28, *28*

R

Reinhard, Johan, *26,* 28, 31, 33

S

shoes, *4, 13, 15,* 47
Simon, Erika and Helmut, 1–2, *6*
snow bridge, 14, *14*
Switzerland
   Porchabella Glacier, 15, *15*
   Rhone Glacier, *53*
   Tortin Glacier, *51*

T

Tatshenshini-Alsek Glacier man, *42,*
   43–47
Theodul Glacier soldier, *9, 13,* 13–14
Thorp, Valerie, *46*
tools
   Andrew Irvine, 38
   Kwäday Dan Ts'ìnchí, 43, 44, *44*
   Ötzi, *3, 3*
tourism, *20, 24, 24,* 25, 51, 53

V

volcanoes, *26,* 31

W

water supply, *50,* 51
weapons, 6, 13, *13*
Wise, Karen, 32

Z

Zárate, Miguel, *26,* 28, *29*